My

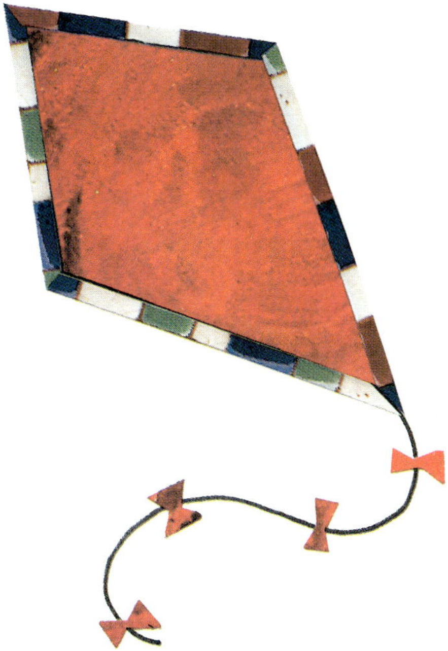

written by
Cynthia Rothman
illustrated by
Sarah Snow

McGraw-Hill
School Division
New York Farmington

My kite flies over the house.

My kite flies over the trees.

My kite flies over the clouds.

My kite flies over the moon.

My kite flies over the mountains.

My kite flies over the sea.

My kite flies home to me.